THE ATMOSPHERE

EARTH'S SPHERES

THE ATMOSPHERE

PLANETARY HEAT ENGINE

GREGORY L. VOGT, Ed.D.

TWENTY-FIRST CENTURY BOOKS · MINNEAPOLIS

Twenty-First Century Books
A division of Lerner Publishing Group
241 First Avenue North
Minneapolis, Minnesota 55401 U.S.A.

Website address: www.lernerbooks.com

Library of Congress Cataloging-in-Publication Data

Vogt, Gregory.
        The atmosphere : planetary heat engine / by Gregory Vogt.
          p.   cm. — (Earth spheres)
        Includes bibliographical references and index.
        ISBN-13: 978-0-7613-2841-4 (lib. bdg. : alk. paper)
        ISBN-10: 0-7613-2841-6 (lib. bdg. : alk. paper)
        1. Atmosphere—Popular works. 2. Weather—Popular works. I. Title.
        II. Series: Vogt, Gregory. Earth's spheres.
        QC863.4.V64 2007
        551.5—dc22   2006007391

Manufactured in the United States of America
1 2 3 4 5 6 – DP – 12 11 10 09 08 07

CONTENTS

THE CONQUEST OF SPACE

In the early 1950s, while the world was still reeling from the effects of World War II (1939–1945) and the Korean War (1950–1953), both the United States and the Soviet Union were conducting rocket experiments and vying to be the first to orbit a satellite around Earth. Meanwhile, California movie studios were off on a new science-fiction moviemaking fad—the conquest of space. They cheerfully cranked out one space movie after another. Rocket ships blasted off to faraway worlds and alien flying saucers came to Earth. The movies were packed with robots, monsters, and special effects. They were fun for their time, but compared to today's movies, with computer-generated effects, the old special effects were primitive. In some films, you could actually see thin wires supporting model rockets and flying saucers!

One special effect of those movies was especially interesting. It was the view of Earth as seen from space. Against a background painting of thousands of stars, Earth appeared as a shiny globe with every continent and ocean clearly seen. It looked pretty real until the first real rockets, with cameras built into their nose cones, took off skyward. These rockets soared hundreds of miles (kilometers) above Earth, tipped over, and fell back. All the while, their onboard cameras took pictures of Earth below. The view was startling. Real Earth didn't look like Earth in the movies. Everywhere you looked, there were clouds. White wisps, cottony patches, long streaks and rows, and giant storm swirls obscured whole continents and broad stretches of Earth's oceans. The rocket-borne cameras not only showed Earth's land and water but its atmosphere too. Earth was far more beautiful and interesting than the moviemakers had imagined.

Due to the modern technology of rocket cameras, Earth-orbiting satellites, super computers, and thousands of weather observers dotted around the globe, we know much more about the envelope of air that surrounds Earth. The atmosphere is a vital and dynamic part of a complex system of interacting spheres that make up the planet. Earth is a sphere, but it is like a painted Russian doll. Open up the outer doll and find a smaller doll inside. Open that one and there is another doll and another.

A picture of Earth taken from outer space shows swirling white clouds encircling the planet.

Inside Earth is a core of metal surrounded by molten and partly molten rock and metal. On top of that is a mantle of hot flowing rock, and above that is a thin lithosphere of surface rock, also called the crust. On top of that are the world's oceans, lakes, and rivers, called the hydrosphere. Intermingled with the hydrosphere is the atmosphere, and within the atmosphere and hydrosphere is the zone of life called the biosphere. Lastly is the thinnest upper layer of the atmosphere, called the exosphere, that stretches out into space and interacts with the energy and particles ejected by the Sun. This book is one in a series of six that tells the story of Earth's spheres. It focuses on the atmosphere, a protective blanket of gases that surrounds the oceans and land of Earth.

CHAPTER 1
AIR

If you made a list of all the things you need for survival, air would be at the top. Everything else, including food, water, clothes, money, and so on, would be of lesser importance. In an emergency, such as getting lost in the wilderness, you can go without food for a week or more and without water for a day or several days if it is not too hot. Air, on the other hand, is something you can't go without for more than a few minutes. Four or five minutes without air and your life is over.

In spite of how important air is to us, air is something we are hardly conscious of. Our planet is surrounded by an atmosphere filled with a mixture of gases we call air. We breathe naturally without reminding ourselves to do so. It is only when we do something like hold our breath and swim underwater or climb a lot of steps that we start concentrating on our breathing. Air is just there. We don't talk or think much about air and the atmosphere, but we do talk about what it does. That's called weather.

WHAT IS AIR?

Air is a mixture of different gases. A gas is one of the three common states of matter that exist on Earth. The other two are solids and liquids. Solids have definite shapes and volume. Liquids have definite volumes, but they flow into and take the shape of the container they are poured into. Gases have neither a definite shape nor a definite volume. If you put air into a container, it will take its shape and fill it completely.

Gas, like all states of matter, consists of very tiny particles called atoms, which are bonded together into slightly larger particles called molecules. Air molecules are so small you could fit 40 sextillion (40 followed by 21 zeros) of them inside a 1-inch (2.5-centimeter) cube. The number is difficult to imagine, but think of M&Ms. If you had 40 sextillion M&Ms, your candy bag would be the size of the Moon.

Molecules inside solids are packed tightly together to form set shapes. Liquid molecules stick to one another but can slide about permitting liquids to change shapes. Gas molecules are separate from one another and can move in all directions and distances.

THE ELEMENTS OF AIR

Atoms are the basic building blocks of the elements that make up our world and the universe. The solid part of Earth consists of elements such as iron, silicon, aluminum, and gold. The oceans are made up of the elements hydrogen and oxygen (combined to form H_2O, or water) with large amounts of salt and other chemicals dissolved in them. Earth's atmosphere is made up primarily of the elements nitrogen (78 percent) and oxygen (21 percent), but it also contains very small amounts of the elements argon, krypton, helium, and hydrogen, and gases such as carbon monoxide, carbon dioxide, and sulfur dioxide.

GASES IN THE ATMOSPHERE

Type of Gas	Percent of the Total Atmosphere
Nitrogen	78
Oxygen	21
Argon	0.9
Carbon dioxide	0.03
Hydrogen, water vapor*, ozone, neon, helium, krypton, xenon	0.07

*The amount of water vapor in the air varies with air temperature. Air at 86°F (30°C) can hold about 220 times the amount of water vapor that air at −40°F (−40°C) can.

The combination of hydrogen and oxygen, which forms liquid water at temperatures between 32°F and 212°F (0°C and 100°C), becomes a gas when evaporated or heated above that range and becomes a solid below that range. Gaseous water in the atmosphere is called water vapor. Solid water is called ice.

UNDER PRESSURE

The molecules in air move very fast, about 1,600 feet (488 meters) per second or 1,090 miles (1,750 kilometers) per hour, at room temperature. If air temperature rises, the molecules move faster, and if it falls, the molecules move slower. Think of air as a three-dimensional pool table where all the balls are moving and bumping into one another constantly. The effect of all this moving and bumping is pressure.

Pressure is a force. A force is defined as a push or a pull. In the case of air pressure, it is just a push. Earth's atmosphere presses on all objects it surrounds, such as your body. It pushes down on your head and shoulders, and it also pushes on your back, stomach, legs, and so on. The amount of pressure is measured in a unit called pounds per square inch or psi (the corresponding metric unit is pascals—newtons per square meter).

On an average day, standing on the seashore (at sea level), the pressure is 14.7 psi (101,000 pascals or 101 kilopascals). That means that a force of 14.7 pounds (6.7 kilograms) pushes on every square inch of your body. You can estimate the atmospheric pressure on your body by estimating how many square inches (centimeters) of skin you have and multiplying it by 14.7 psi. For example, a 12-by-12-inch (930 sq. cm) patch of skin on your chest experiences 2,117 pounds (960 kg), or more than a ton (metric ton) of air pressure! Why don't your lungs collapse? Because your lungs are full of air. The air inside your lungs exerts the same pressure outward as the outside air pressing inward, creating a balance.

If you are wondering how tiny air molecules can produce such pressures, do the following experiment with a bathroom scale and a sack of baseballs. Place one baseball on the scale. It doesn't weigh very much. But if you drop it on the scale, the dial will jump a bit. Drop two balls on the scale, and it will jump a bit more. The baseballs act like giant air molecules hitting the scale's surface. With air, it's not just two molecules. It's sextillions of them hitting the surface at the same moment like a steady downpour of rain. You can mimic this by pouring the entire sack of balls on the scale. As soon as one ball bounces off, another hits it. The dial no longer jumps and falls. It stays high, indicating the pressure of the steady rain of balls landing on it.

One would think we would be constantly aware of this pressure. We are not, because our bodies are made up mostly of water, which is contained in the cells in our bodies. Water does not compress when squeezed.

Because air is a fluid, the pressure it exerts comes from all directions. Everything is in balance and feels normal to you. However, sometimes you can feel air pressure changes when the passageways to the air cavities in your head get blocked. Normally, outside air moves freely in and out of those cavities, but if blocked, a change in outside air pressure can cause the tissues around the cavities to hurt (for example, sinus headache and earache). When the passages open again, air rushes through to balance the pressure. The rush of air causes squeaking and ear "popping" sounds.

Besides the movement of air molecules, there is another reason for the presence of air pressure. The other reason is the weight of air. Hold out your hand. Although you can't see them, your hand is holding sextillions of air molecules. It is not just the molecules touching your skin that you are holding. More molecules are piled on top of those and more on top of those. The pile of molecules in your hand stretches all the way out to space. They add up to a lot of weight pressing on you—about 14.7 pounds (6.7 kg) for every square inch (sq. cm) of your hand.

Air pressure varies in different areas around Earth. If you put a quantity of air inside a jug and seal it with a cork, the air molecules fill the jug and bounce off all inside surfaces of the jug, exerting pressure in all directions. If you place the same amount of air inside a bigger jug, it will fill that jug too, but the pressure inside the larger jug is less because the air molecules are spread out more and have to bounce over a larger surface. In a manner of thinking, Earth's atmosphere is like a giant inside-out jug. Air surrounds Earth's surface and exerts pressure on it because of gravity.

Air pressure is greatest at sea level because of the weight of all the air piled on top, reaching all the way to space. If you rise up into the atmosphere, the air pressure decreases because there is less air above to weigh down on you. If you have ever been on the top of a tall mountain, you know that breathing there is harder because there is less air pressure and the air molecules spread out. If you ride a rocket to space, the outside atmosphere thins out to a few widely spaced stray gas molecules. Nearly all Earth's atmosphere is below you. There is nothing to weigh down on you, and the pressure is essentially zero.

Besides changing altitudes, there are other ways atmospheric pressure changes. In fact, it changes daily around Earth. You can see this using a balloon and a refrigerator. Inflate the balloon and measure how big around it is with a piece of string. Place the balloon in a freezer for several minutes and then measure it again. The balloon will be smaller. Why? The speed of air molecules changes with temperature. Cold air molecules move slower than warm molecules. Because they move more slowly, they exert less pressure on the walls of the balloon and the balloon shrinks. You can take the balloon in the other direction by warming it carefully with a hair dryer. The air molecules will start moving faster, increase the pressure inside, and cause the balloon to expand. If it's heated too much, the balloon will pop.

Although not contained within the rubber of a balloon, Earth's atmosphere expands and contracts with daily

A barometer *(above)* measures Earth's atmospheric pressure. The bellows (the metal disks in the center of the box) expands or contracts with the pressure of the surrounding air. The pointer arm moves up or down with the bellows and records the changes on the graph paper *(at left)*.

changes in temperature. Air is heated by the Sun during the day and cools off during the night. The presence or absence of clouds and the different surfaces (oceans, ice, continents, etc.) beneath the Sun's rays also have a great effect on heating or cooling of the atmosphere. These differences result in widely varying surface temperatures, which warm or cool the air above and change the local pressure.

HOW HIGH?

Space shuttles usually orbit Earth at an altitude of about 200 to 300 miles (300 to 500 km). They are above most of Earth's atmosphere, and the thin traces of the atmosphere

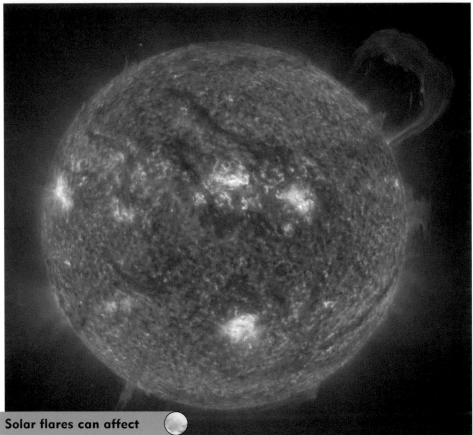

Solar flares can affect Earth's atmosphere and the weather on the ground.

that remain are hardly noticeable. The atmosphere continues to become even thinner the higher you go until it is virtually gone at an altitude of about 600 miles (1,000 km). The upper boundary of the atmosphere varies from time to time, depending on the energy being given off by the Sun. Occasionally, the Sun burps out large amounts of energy from great flares on its surface. If Earth is in the way of those emissions, the atmosphere gets a bit warmer and expands outward to higher elevations.

While orbiting Earth, space shuttle astronauts are treated to beautiful views of Earth's atmosphere. They see the tops of clouds and can watch as major storms cross the oceans. When they look toward the horizon, they are able to see the atmosphere from the side, all the way from the surface to space. Nearest the surface where the air is the thickest, the atmosphere is bright blue with accents of white. The brightness comes from sunlight reflecting off the air molecules and clouds. As the atmosphere thins out toward space, it gets dimmer. The colors become darker blue and violet. Past the outer edges, the atmosphere becomes black. This is where outer space starts. The air is so thin that no light can be seen reflecting off it.

Earth's atmosphere is just a shallow layer of gas that becomes thinner and fainter the higher you go. This picture, taken by an astronaut, shows the Moon just peaking over the upper edge of Earth's atmosphere.

WHY IS THE SKY BLUE?

Just about everybody asks this question at one time or another. But you could also ask why the sky is yellow, red, or purple during sunrise and sunset. The colors you are seeing do not come from the atmosphere. Air is colorless. These are the colors of sunlight. Sunlight is made up of a rainbow of colors including red, orange, yellow, green, blue, indigo, and violet. This is called the visible spectrum. When all those colors are mixed together, the result is white. Take away some of the colors, the result is different. That is what the atmosphere does.

You might think the sky should be white, but something happens as sunlight passes through the atmosphere. On a clear day, with the Sun high in the sky, all the Sun's colors except one pass straight through the atmosphere to Earth's surface. Air molecules bend the path of blue light,

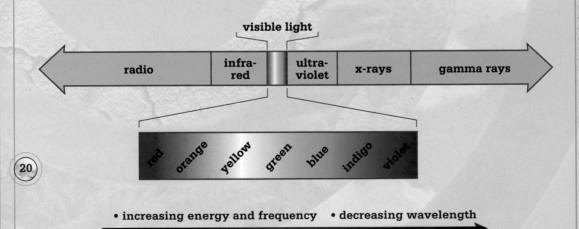

Visible light, or the rainbow colors, are part of a broad spectrum of energy coming to Earth from space. Except for visible light, radio, and parts of infrared and ultraviolet light, most of the spectrum is blocked by Earth's atmosphere.

and it starts zigzagging. This is called scattering. When the blue rays eventually reach the surface, the scattering causes them to come at you from all different directions. This makes the entire sky look blue.

Later in the day, with the Sun low in the west, the sky is yellow and red. The blue color is no longer seen. To reach the surface where you are standing, the rays have to pass through much more air than they did when the Sun was directly overhead. With the Sun low in the sky, yellow light starts scattering. As the Sun lowers further, the rays have to pass through still more air and the yellow is filtered out. The sky reddens as red light starts scattering. Finally, the sky goes black because the Sun is well below the western horizon and Earth has completely blocked out the sunlight. The reverse thing happens to the Sun's colors when the Sun rises in the east. The sky turns to red, yellow, and then blue when the Sun is well above the eastern horizon.

When the Sun is low in the sky, the thicker atmosphere reveals many different sunlight colors.

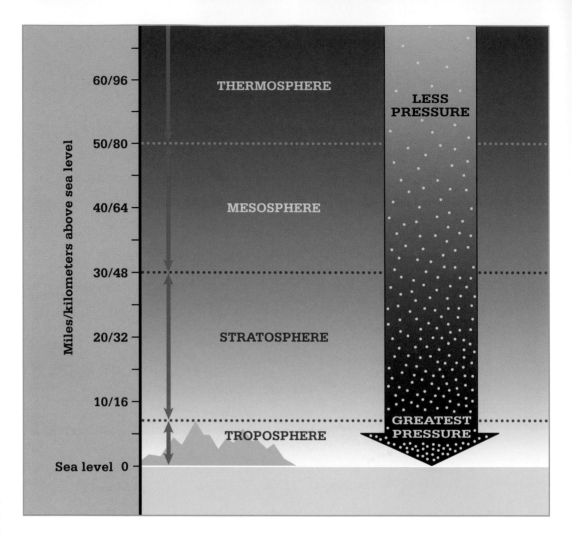

Miles/kilometers above sea level

60/96 — THERMOSPHERE

LESS PRESSURE

50/80 —

40/64 — MESOSPHERE

30/48 —

20/32 — STRATOSPHERE

10/16 —

GREATEST PRESSURE

TROPOSPHERE

Sea level 0 —

LAYERS OF AIR

Earth's atmosphere is divided into four main layers that differ from one another in a variety of ways. Starting at the surface and going upward, they are the troposphere, stratosphere, mesosphere, and thermosphere.

The main thing that changes between the layers is the amount of air present. Because of gravity, air molecules are packed more tightly in the lower layers than in the upper layers. Other differences include air temperature, the gases that are present, and the strength of winds.

The troposphere is the layer of the atmosphere we are most familiar with. This is where Earth's weather happens. All the sunny days and the winter storms take place here. The troposphere stretches up about 7 miles (11 km) above the surface of Earth, although the boundary can vary from 6 to 10 miles (10 to 16 km). Most of the atmosphere's clouds are found here as well. Almost all your life will be spent in the troposphere. The only time you will leave it will be when traveling by jet airliner in the stratosphere, the layer just above the troposphere, or on a space mission should you become an astronaut.

Earth's average temperature at the surface is about 59°F (15°C). If you climb above the surface, the temperature drops about 17°F for every mile (9.4°C for every km). This continues until you reach the top of the troposphere, where the temperature lowers to –61°F (–52°C).

The troposphere contains about 80 percent of Earth's air mass, practically all its water vapor, and most of its clouds. It is where Earth's atmosphere interacts with Earth's hydrosphere, biosphere, and lithosphere. Rain and snow from the troposphere cycles through the oceans and rivers and wears down the land while enabling plants to grow. Wind from the troposphere blows materials around and balances temperatures around the world.

The next layer is called the stratosphere, which extends up to 30 miles (48 km) above Earth's surface.

This is where high-flying jets travel, although most only go a few thousand feet (m) into it. Only the largest storm clouds reach up into the stratosphere.

For the most part, the stratosphere is a quiet layer of the atmosphere with little wind activity. It would seem to be a minor part of Earth's total atmosphere, but it is of major importance to living things on the surface. One of the minor gases found in the stratosphere is ozone. Ozone protects us from a dangerous form of radiation from the Sun—ultraviolet (UV) light.

The temperature of air in the stratosphere increases as you go higher. It starts at −62°F (−52°C) at the bottom of the stratosphere and climbs to a high of −27°F (−33°C) at the top. The heat is generated by the ozone's absorption of the Sun's UV.

The third layer is the mesosphere, which stretches up to about 50 miles (80 km) above the surface. By the time you reach the mesosphere, 99 percent of the atmosphere lies below you.

In spite of the thinness of the air present, the mesosphere is an active place. The mesosphere's molecules are in an excited state because they absorb a great deal of energy from the Sun. The temperature of the mesosphere drops to about −130°F (−90°C) near its top.

Last comes the thermosphere. This layer of air is so thin that once you cross into it, you are considered an astronaut. The thermosphere extends to more than 370 miles (595 km) above Earth. It is the part of the atmosphere that is most intensely affected by the Sun's energy. Temperatures in the thermosphere can reach more than 3,100°F (1,700°C). While this seems extremely hot, the air density is so low that you would hardly notice it. It is like reaching into an oven that is 400°F (200°C). This can be done safely because the air inside doesn't hold much heat. However, the denser cake pan inside holds a lot of heat and will cause burns.

The reason the thermosphere temperature climbs so high is similar to the reason it is much easier to boil a cup of water than to boil a pot of water. More mass can absorb heat. The thermosphere's air has so little mass that it reacts very quickly to changes in the energy output of the Sun. The thicker air below the thermosphere has much more mass and therefore reacts more slowly to energy changes.

The widely separated gas molecules in the thermosphere become electrically charged as the heat and radiation from the Sun break them into ions. In the polar regions of Earth, these ionized gases glow and produce auroras. Auroras, also called the northern and southern lights, are colorful displays of green, yellow, and red lights that sway across the dark night sky.

CHAPTER 2
AIR IN MOTION

Many elementary-school students have had to do the following experiment. Take two thermometers and two cups—one white and one black—and place them in the sunlight. Measure the temperature of the two cups every minute, and plot a graph with the results. Next, put the cups in the shade and again measure the temperature every minute.

There are many variations to this experiment, such as cans instead of cups or lightbulbs instead of the Sun. But the results are always the same. The dark cup heats up faster in the Sun and cools off faster in the shade than the light cup. At the conclusion of the experiment, students are usually asked the question: "What color of clothing is the most comfortable to wear on a hot day?"

There is greater significance to the results of this experiment than just matching light or dark clothes to the daily weather. The ways light and dark surfaces absorb the energy of the Sun is a major driving force within Earth's atmosphere. Most importantly, differences in heating create wind.

CITY TO COUNTRY WIND

Looking at Earth from space, astronauts see a wide range of colors and brightness. Clouds are very white. Oceans are dark blue but occasionally are silvery when sunlight bounces off them at low angles. The land surface ranges through all colors from white snow to black volcanic rock. Pine forests are green, and farmland starts off brown in the spring, turns green in the summer, and becomes golden in the fall. Deserts are tan. Cities are darkish because of roads, parking lots, and dark roofs. Earth is a maze of colors, and each of the colors affects how the Sun's energy is absorbed.

From the results of the school science experiment above, you can guess that the different colors of Earth have important effects on the way Earth absorbs sunlight. Light surfaces reflect most but not all the light that falls on them. For example, clouds and snow reflect up to 95 percent of the sunlight falling on them. Dark surfaces absorb most of the light—about 90 percent—and reflect much less. The light delivers energy from the Sun to the surface and causes the surface to become warm. You are very familiar with this. Remember the last time you

Ice reflects 90 percent of the Sun's heat, while ocean water reflects only 10 percent.

walked across a black asphalt playground or on a sandy beach on a hot summer day? What happens next is important to the atmosphere. The heat absorbed by the surface warms the air directly above it, and that starts the air moving.

In the previous chapter, we learned that molecules in warm air move more rapidly than molecules in cold air. Think of a city surrounded by green farmland and forests. Asphalt streets, parking lots, and dark rooftops of the city absorb much of the Sun's energy during the day. The city becomes hot. The surrounding lighter-colored farm and forestlands absorb less heat and are cooler. (The tradition of going to the country for vacation was partly based on getting away from summer heat spells.)

The different ground temperatures affect air molecules above the city and the country. City air is warmed by the surface, and the air molecules begin moving more rapidly. They collide together with more force and start shoving one another apart. City air becomes less dense and begins to rise upward like a bubble in water. It becomes a vertical wind called an updraft. The rising air reduces the air pressure below.

Meanwhile, air over the surrounding countryside warms, but not as much as the city air. The air molecules there move more slowly and are more densely packed. The countryside air pressure is greater than the pressure over the city. The difference is enough to start a wind flowing into the city to fill the void left by the rising city air. As the country air enters the city, it too becomes warmer and starts to rise, pulling in more country air behind it.

The rising city air eventually cools, and the molecules' movements slow down. The air becomes denser and would fall right back to the surface if it weren't for more warm air pushing up from beneath. Instead, the cooled air spreads out to the sides to become an upper-air wind. The wind flows over the cooler countryside where it falls back to the surface as a downdraft.

The difference between daytime temperatures in the city and the cooler temperatures in the country creates a wind cycle as warm air rises and cooler air rushes in to fill the void. The cycle reverses itself at night.

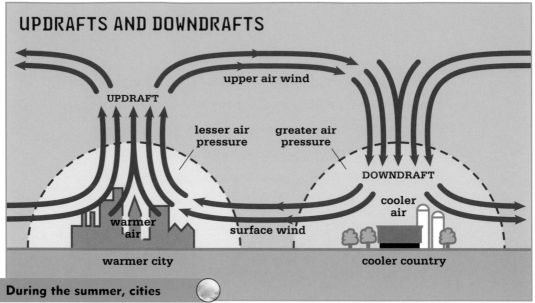

UPDRAFTS AND DOWNDRAFTS

upper air wind

UPDRAFT

lesser air pressure

greater air pressure

DOWNDRAFT

cooler air

warmer air

surface wind

warmer city

cooler country

During the summer, cities become very hot, causing strong updrafts of air. Air over the countryside tends to be much cooler and downdrafts form. This effect causes wind to flow from the country to the city.

Then it flows back to the city to continue the cycle.

When the Sun sets, the city to country to city circulation of air changes. The dark city surface cools off more rapidly than the lighter-colored countryside. Air above the city becomes cooler than the country air. The city air falls while the country air rises. A new wind cycle forms that is reversed from the daytime cycle.

LAND AND SEA BREEZES

The cycling of wind is much more complicated than just presented. Many more factors come into play. For example, the altitude of the land surface makes a big difference. Air over a range of snowcapped mountains becomes very chilled not only because the white snow reflects most of the sunlight but also because of altitude.

Air temperature drops about 17°F (9.4°C) for every mile (km) you climb up into the troposphere. Air over mountaintops becomes very cold and starts falling down the mountain flanks like a river of air. Then it blows out over the surrounding plains. On the other hand, if one of the mountains is an erupting volcano, tremendous hot-air currents are generated that create strong updrafts flowing up the volcano's side.

The presence of a mountain range can deflect surface winds into new directions. But mountains aren't the only things that block wind. Downtown streets in big cities are often lined with tall buildings. The buildings deflect and focus wind currents so that they are

Moist, offshore winds are deflected upward by the volcanoes of the Kurile Island chain along the Pacific Ocean coast of Russia. Air cools as it rises up and over the mountains, causing moisture to condense into clouds and rain.

FASTEST WIND EVER

Wind speeds vary across Earth. Some places seem to get more than their share of wind. Saint Paul Island in Alaska has an average annual wind speed of 18 miles (30 km) per hour. Los Angeles, California, is much calmer at an annual 6 miles (10 km) per hour. Go to Mount Washington, New Hampshire, and hang on to your hat. The average speed at the summit—6,262 feet (1,909 m)—is 35 miles (56 km) per hour. Mount Washington also holds the world wind speed record of 231 miles (372 km) per hour! That is about twice as fast as a hurricane wind. The only thing faster is the wind in some rare monster tornadoes that can reach 300 miles (483 km) per hour.

sometimes strong enough to blow pedestrians into the street.

When we examined the dark city/light country example, we treated it as an isolated place to make it easier to understand the airflow processes. That is not the way it is in real life. The landscape is dotted with cities, forests, farms, deserts, mountains, lakes, oceans, snow and ice fields, and so on. Each has its own properties for absorbing and giving off the Sun's energy. A surface wind produced in one location may collide with a wind from a different location moving in a different direction. These winds may combine, block, or divert one another. This gets pretty complicated, but there are even more factors at play.

AS THE WORLD TURNS

If Earth were just a smooth sphere covered entirely with an ocean, wind patterns would be easy to understand. The Sun's heating of the equator region would cause warm air to rise and spread to the North and South poles where it would cool down and fall back to the surface. There would be two winds. High-altitude winds would flow from the equator straight to the poles, and surface winds would flow straight from the poles to the equator. From the side, these wind patterns would look like flattened circles.

With a wind system like that, weather forecasting would be simple. Every day the forecast would be the same: "Expect strong northerly winds in the morning followed by southerly winds in the afternoon." But Earth is

NAMING WINDS

It can be confusing when TV weather forecasters report the direction the wind is blowing. When they say there is a north wind, they are saying the wind is coming from the north, not blowing toward the north. Winds are named for the directions from which they come and not the directions they are going. The reason for this is a device called a weather vane.

A weather vane is a horizontal arrow that pivots on a stick when wind blows. The arrowhead is small and the feather large. When the wind blows, the feather catches more wind and is blown away. The arrowhead points into the wind. The compass direction in which the arrowhead points gives the wind its name.

Earth's rotation is demonstrated here in a time-lapse photograph of the stars in the night sky over Gzhel, Russia. The stars are fixed, but Earth's rotation makes them look as if they are moving in circles around a point in the sky directly over Earth's North Pole.

not that simple. Continents and mountains interrupt the basic circulation patterns, and an even bigger force is at work. Earth rotates.

Earth spins once every twenty-four hours. This rotation causes objects on the equator to travel eastward at about 1,000 miles (1,600 km) per hour. Objects north and south of the equator travel in smaller circles, so they don't move as fast. By the time you reach the North and South poles, the speed drops down to 0 miles (km) per hour. These speed differences across Earth's surface deflect surface winds.

To understand what is happening, we need some sort of marker to tell us how air is moving. A flag, waving in the wind, indicates wind direction. That's good for checking on local winds, but how do you know what wind is doing around the world? You would need a lot of flags.

A good way of telling what is happening to the wind is to observe clouds from space. Clouds move with the wind. Pictures of the clouds, taken by satellites, show what clouds and the wind blowing them are doing over Earth's entire surface. Predominant wind patterns flow to the east or to the west. Clouds within those patterns tend to move in broad swirls that can span whole countries and sometimes whole continents. Downdrafts of air in the atmosphere spiral in a clockwise direction, as seen from above, while updrafts spiral in a counterclockwise direction. That only happens to Northern Hemisphere air.

A satellite photograph, pieced together to show North and South America, Europe, Asia, Africa, Australia, and Antarctica, shows the cloud patterns influenced by Earth's rotation as well as other weather conditi

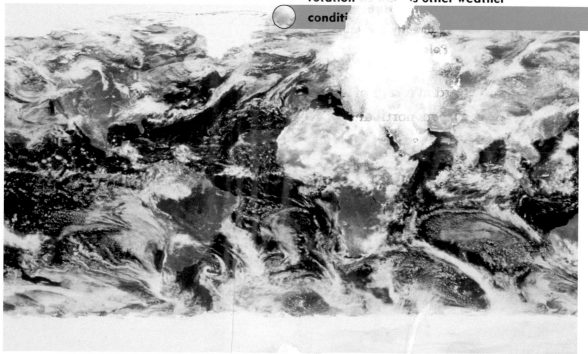

Southern Hemisphere air spirals in the opposite direction. Earth's rotation creates the predominant winds and swirls. The spiraling phenomenon is called the Coriolis effect.

To help you understand the Coriolis effect, you will need a world globe that spins on a stand, a dry erase marker, plastic wrap, and a friend. First, cover the globe with plastic wrap, because you are going to draw marks on it and want them to come off afterward. Next, hold the marker near the globe's North Pole and along the metal ring of the stand that surrounds the globe. Use this ring like a ruler for drawing a line. With the globe still, run the marker along the ring from the North Pole to the equator. This makes a straight line.

When you draw a line from the North Pole to the equator, the line will curve as the globe is turned to simulate Earth's rotation. This is called the Coriolis effect.

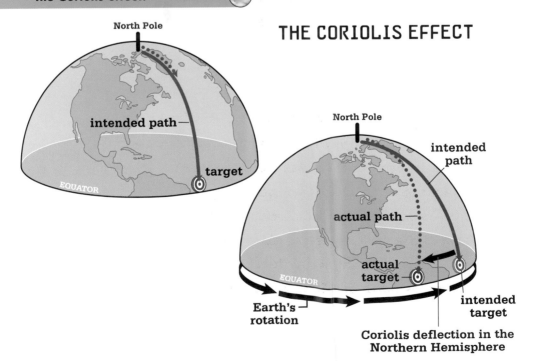

THE CORIOLIS EFFECT

North Pole

intended path —

target

EQUATOR

North Pole

intended path

actual path —

actual target —

intended target

Earth's rotation

EQUATOR

Coriolis deflection in the Northern Hemisphere

Then, draw another line from the North Pole. Have your friend slowly turn the globe from west to east to simulate Earth's rotation. The second line curves to the west at the equator. Last, draw a third line with the globe moving. This time, start at the equator and go to the North Pole. This line has an eastward curve at the equator. Repeat this experiment with the Southern Hemisphere (South Pole to equator and equator to South Pole). These curved lines will be just the opposite of the Northern Hemisphere lines. This is the Coriolis effect.

Whenever wind blows in a direction that is not parallel to Earth's equator, Earth's motion curves its path over the surface. Surface and upper-air winds move about Earth in large spiraling patterns. Spirals collide and rub against one another to complicate things. On occasion, really powerful spirals are created. Hurricanes and tornadoes are spiraling storms of tremendous power.

WORLDWIDE WINDS

Although Earth's weather is constantly jumbled with local weather systems, large wind patterns cross its entire surface. The direction of these wind patterns is related to their latitude north or south of the equator. From 30 degrees north to 30 degrees south, the wind generally blows from the east to the west. These are the trade winds. West winds, called prevailing westerlies, blow from 30 degrees to 60 degrees north and 30 to 60 degrees south.

From 60 degrees north to the North Pole and 60 degrees south to the South Pole, winds are eastward again and circle the Arctic and Antarctic. They are called the polar easterlies. The winds are usually better defined in the Southern Hemisphere because there are fewer landmasses to disrupt airflow with friction. South of the tip of South America, prevailing westerlies can blow entirely around Earth without once crossing land.

Friction does occur between the winds themselves. For example, at 30 degrees north and 30 degrees south, the tropical easterlies run

Prevailing winds, named for the direction from which they come, flow around Earth in wide bands. They are called prevailing winds because they almost always flow in the same direction.

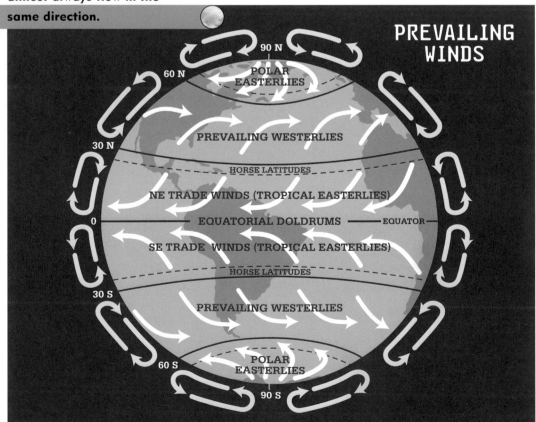

PREVAILING WINDS

90 N
60 N
POLAR EASTERLIES
30 N
PREVAILING WESTERLIES
HORSE LATITUDES
NE TRADE WINDS (TROPICAL EASTERLIES)
0
EQUATORIAL DOLDRUMS — EQUATOR
SE TRADE WINDS (TROPICAL EASTERLIES)
30 S
HORSE LATITUDES
PREVAILING WESTERLIES
60 S
POLAR EASTERLIES
90 S

alongside but in the opposite direction of the prevailing westerlies. Friction between the two opposite air masses jumbles the air and creates a narrow band of clouds and thunderstorms that can encircle the globe.

Although these bands can have stormy air, they can also be very calm. Early sailors dreaded getting caught there with no wind to puff out their sails. Sometimes ships from Spain, carrying horses to the New World, became becalmed. When freshwater supplies began to run out, horses were thrown overboard. Other ships passing through these latitudes reported seas strewn with the bodies of dead horses. Sailors called these areas the horse latitudes.

JETTING ACROSS THE CONTINENT

Airline pilots are careful about plotting their courses on long-distance flights. Instead of flying in a straight line from San Francisco, California, to Washington, D.C., they may choose a route that passes over the northern states. In spite of the extra distance, they arrive sooner and use less fuel. What they are doing is taking advantage of a unique wind called the jet stream.

Jet streams are powerful easterly winds that flow like rivers of air near the boundary of the troposphere and the stratosphere. These winds are usually about 600 miles (970 km) across. If a pilot can get into the jet stream and follow its course, the airplane will get a strong tail wind. The pilot

WINDCHILL INDEX

A 15-mile-per-hour (24-km) wind might not seem like much until it is winter. If the air temperature is 30°F (−1°C), the wind causes it to feel like it is only 19°F (−7°C). That's because moving air carries away body heat more quickly than still air. The faster the wind, the colder it feels.

The chart below comes from the National Weather Service. The dark blue areas indicate windchill temperatures at which exposed skin will suffer frostbite in fifteen minutes or less.

Temperature (°F)

Calm	40	35	30	25	20	15	10	5	0	-5	-10	-15	-20	-25	-30	-35	-40	-45
5	36	31	25	19	13	7	1	-5	-11	-16	-22	-28	-34	-40	-46	-52	-57	-63
10	34	27	21	15	9	3	-4	-10	-18	-22	-28	-35	-41	-47	-53	-59	-66	-72
15	32	25	19	13	6	0	-7	-13	-19	-26	-32	-39	-45	-51	-58	-64	-71	-77
20	30	24	17	11	4	-2	-9	-15	-22	-29	-35	-42	-48	-55	-61	-68	-74	-81
25	29	23	16	9	3	-4	-11	-17	-24	-31	-37	-44	-51	-58	-64	-71	-78	-84
30	28	22	15	8	1	-5	-12	-19	-26	-33	-39	-46	-53	-60	-67	-73	-80	-87
35	28	21	14	7	0	-7	-14	-21	-27	-34	-41	-48	-55	-62	-69	-76	-82	-89
40	27	20	13	6	-1	-8	-15	-22	-29	-35	-43	-50	-57	-64	-71	-78	-84	-91
45	26	19	12	5	-2	-9	-16	-23	-30	-37	-44	-51	-58	-65	-72	-79	-86	-93
50	26	19	12	4	-3	-10	-17	-24	-31	-38	-45	-52	-60	-67	-74	-81	-88	-95
55	25	18	11	4	-3	-11	-18	-25	-32	-39	-46	-54	-61	-68	-75	-82	-89	-97
60	25	17	10	3	-4	-11	-19	-26	-33	-40	-48	-55	-62	-69	-76	-84	-91	-98

Wind speed (mph)

can save 500 gallons (2,000 liters) of expensive jet fuel on the trip. Flying the other way, however, the pilot will do his or her best to stay out of the jet stream because the stream will slow the plane and make it use more fuel.

Jet streams occur in both the Northern Hemisphere and Southern Hemisphere. They are created by strong

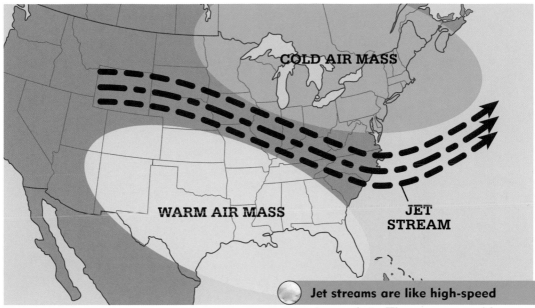

COLD AIR MASS

WARM AIR MASS

JET STREAM

Jet streams are like high-speed rivers of air. They are caused by strong high-altitude pressure differences in the air. In winter, jet streams are more powerful because of greater air temperature differences in the north and south. In summer, with milder temperatures, slower jet streams tend to cross the continent farther north.

high-altitude air pressure differences between one area and another. A river of air is created that snakes across the country between these pressure zones. If you were to take a slice across a jet stream, you would see that it is like a tunnel. Wind moves at about 80 to 100 miles (130 to 160 km) per hour around the outsides of the tunnel. Winds reaching up to 190 miles (300 km) per hour are found in the middle.

Jet streams are stronger in winter because of greater air temperature differences across the continent, which leads to greater pressure differences. Cold air masses from the north (in the Northern Hemisphere) tend to warp the jet stream's course to the south across the middle United States. In summer the jet stream weakens and flows across southern Canada.

CHAPTER 3

WEATHER IN OUR LIVES

Earth's atmosphere is like a giant engine that moves air, heat, and water around Earth's surface. The effect of the engine is to moderate worldwide temperatures. It is an impossible job to do completely. Earth's surface is made up of many different materials that react in their own ways to the Sun's heat.

Heat differences create high and low pressures, and those create winds that flow from one place to another. Balance is never achieved because of surface differences and because Earth rotates. Each change in the atmosphere triggers another change, which triggers another change, and so on. It's pretty complicated. The effect of all this change is what we call weather. Weather is simply what Earth's atmosphere is doing at a particular place at a particular moment.

WATER IN THE SKY

Earth's spheres are constantly interacting. One of the most powerful interactions is the movement of water through the atmosphere, hydrosphere, biosphere, and lithosphere. Ocean and lake water, resting on Earth's surface, evaporates into the atmosphere to become water vapor. It is spread by the winds to all parts of Earth. Eventually, the water vapor condenses back into liquid or solid form and falls to the surface as rain or snow.

Upon the land, water collects in streams and rivers and flows over the surface or soaks into the soil. Some water is absorbed by the roots of plants and returned to the atmosphere by green leaves during the plant growth process called photosynthesis. Regardless of its course, all water eventually returns to lakes and oceans to evaporate and start the process again. This interaction of water is called the hydrologic cycle.

Interesting things happen when water changes. We usually say water changes when it goes from solid to liquid and from liquid to gas and back again. Water can also go directly from solid to gas and gas to solid.

As a solid, water has a crystal form. The water molecules organize into a hexagonal, or six-sided, pattern. When warmed to the melting point, individual water

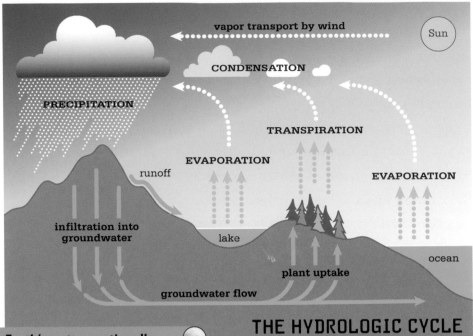

vapor transport by wind

Sun

CONDENSATION

PRECIPITATION

TRANSPIRATION

runoff

EVAPORATION

EVAPORATION

infiltration into
groundwater

lake

ocean

plant uptake

groundwater flow

THE HYDROLOGIC CYCLE

Earth's water continually recycles itself from the land and ocean and back to the atmosphere. When there is enough moisture in the air, precipitation (rain or snow) will fall to Earth's surface, where it collects in lakes and oceans or seeps into the soil. Through evaporation or transpiration of water by plants, the water returns to the atmosphere only to fall back to Earth again.

molecules separate from the crystal structure but still cling together as a liquid. If warmed further, the molecules may completely separate from the liquid and become water vapor. This is called evaporation.

If you apply lots of heat to water and cause it to boil, you can see water change to gas. Take a hot shower to reverse the process. The air in the bathroom becomes very humid. As the water vapor comes in contact with the cool bathroom mirror, it condenses. Something similar happens on warm nights. Water drops condense on cool grass blades to make dew.

However, when ice melts, you don't always see liquid water. A clump of snow on a sidewalk can gradually disappear without water running off. This happens because the snow is warmed by sunlight, but the air surrounding it is still cold and dry. Water molecules go directly from ice into vapor. The process is called sublimation.

The word *sublimation* is also used for the process in which water vapor turns directly into a solid. If you live in cold country, you will sometimes wake to find the ground covered with frost. Overnight, the ground was very cold. When moist air drifted above the ground, water molecules brushing over the surface clung to it and froze. The same kind of thing happens inside some freezers. Open the freezer and

Water vapor formed ice crystals on these leaves during a cold night. The process of going from solid to gas or from gas to solid is called sublimation.

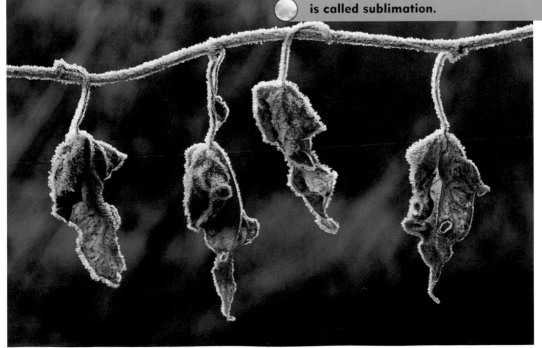

let in warm, moist air from your house. The next time you open the freezer, the water vapor will have converted directly into frost that lines the walls and food packages. These changes in water, while in the atmosphere, lead to many interesting phenomena, including clouds, rain, and snow.

CLOUDS

Water in the form of water vapor makes up 0 to 4 percent of the atmosphere. Water vapor is what you get when oceans, rivers, and lakes evaporate. It is what you get when plants give off water from their leaves into the atmosphere (which is called transpiration). Water vapor is also created inside a boiling kettle. Water vapor is invisible, but when the vapor leaves the kettle, it immediately starts to cool and becomes steamy clouds of very tiny drops of liquid water. This process is called condensation.

You can tell water vapor is present in the air through condensation. To see condensation at work, fill a glass with ice water and set it in a saucer. In a few minutes, water drops will form on the outside of the glass. Water vapor from the atmosphere comes into contact with the cold sides of the glass. Warm air holds more water vapor than cold air. Air near the icy glass becomes cold, and the water vapor molecules attach themselves to the outside of the glass. Microscopic water drops merge and soon become water drops big enough to see.

Cumulus clouds fill a bright blue sky. Composed of droplets of water surrounding dust particles, clouds provide clues as to how the weather will change.

What does this have to do with clouds? Earth's atmosphere has vast amounts of tiny dust particles that come from volcanic eruptions, forest fires, dust storms, and human-made pollution. Air currents waft the particles through the atmosphere so that the dust is well mixed within the air. When air is cool, water vapor condenses on the outside of the dust particles. At first, the drops are microscopic, but nearby drops join together. Eventually, the drops get large enough to be seen. When you see a cloud, you are seeing trillions upon trillions of water drops clinging to dust.

As long as the drops do not become too big, air currents will keep the droplets floating. The currents shove

and pinch and stretch the clouds into an amazing array of shapes. Scattered puffy clouds usually accompany a nice day. A broad layer of clouds overhead, especially one that appears to be getting lower, indicates a change in the weather such as a storm. Giant clusters of boiling clouds that seem to reach to the top of the sky become powerful thunderstorms. Layered clouds that are getting higher indicate better weather on the way.

However, not all clouds are made up of drops of liquid water. Clouds in winter and very high clouds, where the air temperature is very low, are made up of tiny ice crystals. Ice crystals sometimes produce beautiful effects when moonlight hits them. During a full moon, the moonlight may reflect off ice crystals and form a beautiful halo completely surrounding the Moon.

FALLING WATER

Clouds are a delicate balance of water droplets, temperature, and air currents. If too much water condenses on dust particles, they will fall. If the air temperature drops, the atmosphere will not be able to hold as much water vapor as before. Then rain will fall.

When clouds release their water, it falls to the ground as precipitation in the form of rain and snow. If the air near Earth's surface is warmer than the freezing point of water, the water will be in liquid form as it reaches the ground. If the air temperature is below freezing, the droplets will become solid. On occasion, the falling water will start out as rain but freeze on the way down. Then it is called sleet. If the drops freeze solid, they become ice pellets.

Hailstones are another form of frozen water. Rain starts falling during a thunderstorm, but it gets caught by strong updrafts that carry it up to higher altitudes where it freezes. It starts falling again as more water condenses on the outside of it. Once more, it is caught and carried upward and the new water freezes to form a layer surrounding the ice core. This can happen several times, making hailstones multilayered like an onion. Hailstones can be like small marbles, or they can grow to golf-ball size.

The largest hailstone ever recorded in the United States fell in Nebraska in 2003. It measured 7 inches (17.8 cm) in diameter.

METEOROLOGY

Meteorology is the science of Earth's atmosphere and its weather. When you watch a television weather forecast, the first thing the forecaster does is tell you what the weather is like that very moment. It is raining or snowing or hot and sunny or cold and windy. Then the forecaster tells you what to expect next. A meteorologist is a weather scientist.

The tools of the meteorologist are many. But in the early days, the only tools available were thermometers, wind gauges, barometers, rain gauges, and psychrometers. Thermometers tell the temperature of the air at any particular moment. Wind gauges measure wind speed and direction. Barometers measure air pressure, and rain gauges count up how much rain has fallen. Psychrometers measure the amount of water vapor in the air.

Modern, electronic versions of these tools are still used today. The data they collect are radioed or sent by the Internet to central computers that compile data from stations around the world. This gives meteorologists regional and worldwide views of the weather. Knowing from experience the direction that air masses are likely to move, meteorologists can forecast the coming weather.

Other more advanced tools are also available for studying the weather. Doppler radar uses a transmitter to send radio waves into the atmosphere. When the waves hit particles suspended in the air, especially those in clouds heavily laden with moisture, the waves bounce back to a receiver antenna. The receiver collects the

YOUR OWN WEATHER STATION

What's the weather going to be like today? You can turn on the TV or go to the Internet to find out the temperature and wind conditions of your hometown, but the numbers may not be accurate for your exact location. You might live where there are a lot of trees, in a narrow valley, or on a hilltop. It will be colder or warmer where you are, windier or calmer, and so on. If you want accurate numbers, you have to do it yourself.

Many people have their own backyard weather stations. They can be as simple as an outdoor thermometer or more complex with weather vanes, anemometers, recording thermometers, and automatic rain gauges. Some weather hobbyists even build their own weather instruments. Check out the references at the end of this book to learn more.

Weather studies make great science fair projects. If you really enjoy it, you may even join a weather network and send your measurements to your local TV weather forecaster to announce during daily forecasts.

waves and uses them to map the location of the clouds, their velocity, and their direction of movement. These maps appear on computer screens.

Weather satellites in space take pictures of the world's clouds. Satellites, placed in high stationary orbits, can take pictures of nearly one-third of Earth's surface at a time. Cloud patterns show up beautifully in the pictures

Meteorologists use computers and satellite imagery to track storms as well as local weather patterns.

and indicate the weather in diverse locations. Satellites also carry instruments that can measure temperatures, wind speeds, and even the composition of the air, such as the amount of ozone present.

BATTLE OF THE FRONTS

One thing meteorologists watch for is the passage of fronts. A front is the boundary between two air masses with different temperatures, pressures, densities, and humidity levels. Air masses are like huge bubbles in the troposphere. One air mass might be as big as the United States and contain warm, humid air. Another might contain cold, dry air.

When air masses collide, a battle takes place. One air mass tries to shove the other aside. If warm air is doing the shoving, the battle line is called a warm front. If cold air is shoving, the battle line is called a cold front. Sometimes the two masses are equally matched and neither

The top picture shows a cold front, in which a cold and denser air mass pushes under a less dense warm air mass. The lower picture shows a warm front, in which a warm air mass rides up and over a cold air mass. Clouds and rain often form along the fronts.

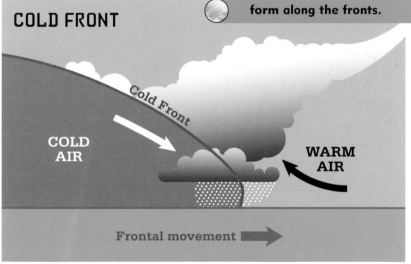

COLD FRONT

Cold Front

COLD AIR

WARM AIR

Frontal movement

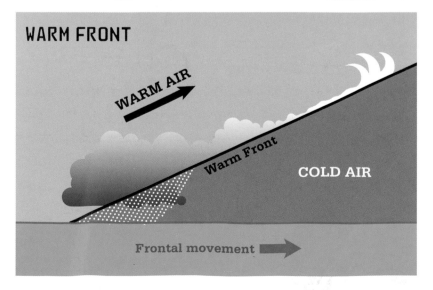

WARM FRONT

WARM AIR

Warm Front

COLD AIR

Frontal movement

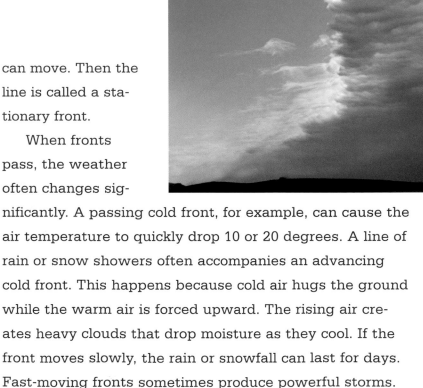

Clouds mark the collision between a warm front and a cold front. A warm air mass on the left is being shoved up and over the cooler air mass on the right. Moisture in the warm air is condensing to form clouds and rain.

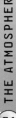

can move. Then the line is called a stationary front.

When fronts pass, the weather often changes significantly. A passing cold front, for example, can cause the air temperature to quickly drop 10 or 20 degrees. A line of rain or snow showers often accompanies an advancing cold front. This happens because cold air hugs the ground while the warm air is forced upward. The rising air creates heavy clouds that drop moisture as they cool. If the front moves slowly, the rain or snowfall can last for days. Fast-moving fronts sometimes produce powerful storms.

A warm front usually brings milder weather that may last for many days. In the summer, when the temperatures are especially warm, a warm front can bring hot, stifling air that makes it uncomfortable to be outside.

EXTREME STORMS

If Earth were a uniform sphere that didn't rotate, its weather would be uniform too. The day side would be hot and the night side cold. But Earth is anything but uniform. Some pretty extreme weather occurs when all the conditions are just right. Major storms erupt and cause extensive wind and flood damage to cities, forests, and farmlands. These storms include thunderstorms, tornadoes, and hurricanes. The driving factor for all of them is strong updrafts.

Thunderstorms get their name from the booming sound created when lightning strikes. These are powerful, fast-moving storms that are about 5 to 10 miles (8 to 16 km) across. The clouds are dark and heavy and boil upward. They may stretch into the stratosphere. Thunderstorms have strong winds and often drop rain so rapidly that drivers sometimes have to pull their cars over to the roadside because they can't see. Electrical charges build up in the clouds and the ground below, causing massive discharges called lightning.

A thunderstorm begins its life as a warm, moist air mass rising from the ground. The air cools, and somewhere between 10,000 and 20,000 feet (3,000 to 6,000 m), the moisture condenses, causing billowing clouds. The updrafts continue, and clouds grow and rise 40,000 feet (12,000 m) or more above the surface. Microscopic water droplets join and grow into large raindrops or ice crystals. When the raindrops or crystals get too large for the updraft to support, they fall. As they fall, they drag air with them and create strong downdrafts next to the updrafts. The wind slams into Earth's surface and spreads out as strong, swirling winds. The storm may produce pounding rain in summer or blizzards in winter.

Tornadoes are tightly spinning storms that produce a vacuum-cleaner-like vortex sucking up dust and dirt, ripping out trees by the roots, flinging cars and trailers, and blowing apart buildings. Tornadoes form funnel shapes that can be tight and twisting (hence the nickname twister) with a base a few tens of yards wide, or they can be broad cones with a base as much as 1 mile (1.6 km) across. The base of the cone may never reach down to the ground. In that case, the tornado is called a funnel cloud.

When a tornado passes over water, it sucks the water and is called a waterspout.

This tornado touched down near Jayton, Texas, in May 2005.

A satellite image of **Hurricane Katrina shows the storm bearing down on Louisiana and Mississippi in September 2005.**

Meteorologists are still struggling to understand the mechanism that causes tornadoes to spin. They know that very strong updrafts, temperature differences, and winds colliding from different directions are all involved.

Hurricanes (called typhoons, or tropical cyclones, in other parts of the world) are Earth's most powerful storms. They are typically 100 to 300 miles (160 to 500 km) across, but the biggest hurricanes can cover thousands of square miles at a time and disrupt and threaten the lives of millions of people.

The hurricane season in the Northern Hemisphere usually begins in June and ends in November. The warm ocean water—at least 80°F (27°C)—heats moist surface air, causing it to rise. While rising, the air starts to cool and the water starts condensing into cloud droplets. During condensation, heat contained in the water is

In 2005 Hurricane Katrina's powerful winds tore homes to pieces in New Orleans, Louisiana. Heavy rain and giant storm waves pushed so much water into nearby Lake Pontchartrain that the lake overflowed its levees. This caused extensive flooding in the city.

released into the air, powering strong updrafts. Clouds form and start swirling as the Coriolis effect takes hold. The fledgling storm is called a tropical depression because of low pressures at its middle. When winds exceed 39 miles (63 km) per hour, the storm is reclassified as a tropical storm. If wind speeds climb above 74 miles (120 km) per hour, the storm is reclassified again as a hurricane.

In spite of their destructive nature, hurricanes are a vital part of the heat engine of Earth's atmosphere. They help balance the worldwide temperatures by moving and spreading warm air and cycling huge amounts of water through the atmosphere. Hurricanes are like pressure release valves for the atmosphere.

CHAPTER 4

THE CLIMATE IS CHANGING

Earth's atmosphere is a dynamic system. The atmosphere changes one moment to the next all over Earth. Short-lived changes are called weather. Knowing what the weather is like at any moment is useful for planning your day. Long-term changes are different. For example, the weather in Fairbanks, Alaska, can get quite warm. A hot day in Fairbanks can reach 100°F (38°C). If you like hot weather, Fairbanks might look like a great place to live, except for one problem. The temperature there can also drop to –40°F (–40°C) during a winter that never seems to end. When people make a decision on where to live, they don't just look at the daily weather but also at the long-term picture.

59

PASSING SEASONS

The most familiar long-term change in the atmosphere is the passage of the seasons—cold and windy in winter, wet and mild in spring, hot and humid in summer, dry and balmy in the fall. Many people think Earth's seasons are caused by how far Earth is from the Sun—closer in summer and farther in winter. However, have you ever wondered what the weather is like down under in Australia? Use the Internet to check it out.

You will learn that when it is winter in the United States (Northern Hemisphere country), it is summer in Australia (Southern Hemisphere country) and vice versa. Since different parts of Earth experience summer and winter at the same time, something other than distance to the Sun must create the seasons. What is really happening? Let's look at how the Sun appears to move in summer and winter.

The summer Sun in the Northern Hemisphere rises in the northeast, crosses high in the sky, and sets in the northwest. Daylight lasts for many hours. The winter Sun rises in the southeast, crosses low in the sky, and sets in the southwest. The hours of daylight are fewer. This is important to understanding the seasons.

On the day side of Earth, sunlight heats the surface. On the night side, the heat radiates back into space. Longer summer daytime hours cause the surface to gain more heat in the day than it loses at night. On the other hand, longer winter nighttime hours cause the surface to lose more heat at night than it gains during the day. Hours of heating are a significant factor for creating Earth's seasons, but there is another factor—the angle of the sunlight.

Find a flashlight and go into a darkened room. Face a wall straight on and shine the light. The light will form a bright circle on the wall. While aiming the light at the same place, walk to the side so that the light strikes at an angle. This spreads the light out. No spot under the light receives as much energy as it did before.

In the middle of a summer day, sunlight comes down at a steep angle and its energy is concentrated. If you were to stand barefoot on a sandy beach at noon in the middle of summer, the Sun would be almost directly over your head. Your shadow would be small and the sand very hot. In winter the Sun would be lower in the sky at noon. Your shadow would be longer and the sand beneath your feet cold.

Earth's seasons are the result of the combination of the hours of daylight and the angle of the Sun's rays. Long hours of daylight and direct rays create summer. Short hours of daylight and slanted rays create winter. Halfway in between summer and winter is spring and fall. Now we get to the big question. Why does this happen?

Earth is like a top that spins 365.25 times every year. The spin takes place around an imaginary line called the axis. The ends of the axis are the North and South poles. The axis is tilted 23.5 degrees to the path of Earth's orbit. The axis points the same direction no matter where Earth is on its orbit. It is this tilt of Earth's axis that causes changes in the

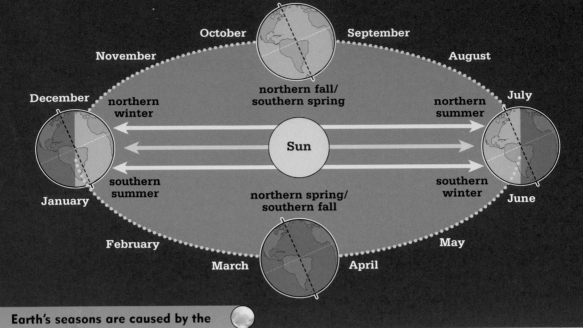

October

September

November

August

December

northern
winter

July

northern
fall/
southern spring

northern
summer

Sun

January

southern
summer

June

southern
winter

February

May

northern spring/
southern fall

March

April

Earth's seasons are caused by the **tilt of Earth's axis as it orbits the Sun. In summer the tilt causes sunlight to be more direct and the days to be longer than in winter. In spring and fall, the days are of equal length and sunlight is spread out equally from the North Pole to the South Pole.**

amount of heat Earth's hemispheres receive during the seasons.

For part of the orbit, the North Pole leans in the direction of the Sun. Hours of daylight are long, and the Sun is high overhead. This creates summer in the Northern Hemisphere. At the same time, the South Pole leans away from the Sun. The Sun is low in the sky, and the hours of daylight are fewer. This creates winter in the Southern Hemisphere. Six months later, with Earth on the opposite side of the Sun, the North Pole leans away from the Sun— winter in the Northern Hemisphere—while the South Pole leans toward the Sun—summer in the Southern Hemisphere.

What about spring and fall? Halfway between summer and winter, neither pole of Earth leans toward the Sun. Both hemispheres have the same amount of daylight, and the angle of sunlight is the same. Temperatures fall between the extremes of summer and winter.

CLIMATE

While the range of the weather during the seasons is a good indicator of what a place is like, meteorologists look at an even longer-term picture of the weather. This long-term picture is called the climate. It is the average weather for a location generally taken over a thirty-year period. The long period is used so that all the extreme days balance one another out. Fairbanks's average year-round temperature, for example, is about 28°F (−2.2°C). But there is more to climate than just temperature. Climate also includes precipitation, sunny versus cloudy days, and so on.

Knowing about the climate is very useful because it tells us about the health of the atmosphere. If the average temperature stays pretty much the same year after year and so does rain and snowfall, you might say things are going well. However, if the temperature average starts climbing and stays that way for several years, a warming trend is taking place. When the climate starts changing, important events can occur.

GLOBAL WARMING

Over the past few decades, a disturbing trend in the atmosphere has taken place. The atmosphere is getting warmer. The problem is called global warming, and it spells potential trouble for everyone. The idea behind global warming is that natural and human-made activities are increasing the amount of the Sun's heat that Earth retains. Natural activities include forest fires and volcanic eruptions that kick up lots of dust and carbon dioxide into the atmosphere. Human activities include chemical pollution and the burning of oil, coal, and natural gas that releases carbon dioxide and other gases.

Forest fires and volcanoes have always existed, but human-generated pollution is a relatively new factor. With the world population growing rapidly and the explosive growth in the use of fuels and chemicals, the chemical composition of Earth's atmosphere is changing. The amount of carbon dioxide, for example, has increased 30 percent since the 1700s, when burning coal for factories and homes became common.

Carbon dioxide is a greenhouse gas. This means that the gas acts like the glass in a greenhouse to trap the Sun's heat. Carbon dioxide is a natural component of the atmosphere, and without its heat-trapping effect, Earth's average temperature would drop about 60°F (30°C). The problem is the extra carbon dioxide and other greenhouse gases

The United States has only 5 percent of the world's population but is responsible for 25 percent of the carbon dioxide released into the atmosphere every year.

THE GREENHOUSE EFFECT

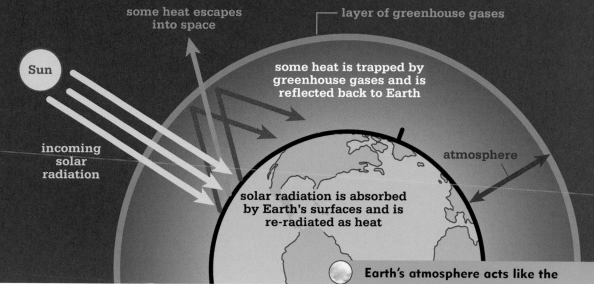

some heat escapes
into space

layer of greenhouse gases

some heat is trapped by
greenhouse gases and is
reflected back to Earth

Sun

incoming
solar
radiation

atmosphere

solar radiation is absorbed
by Earth's surfaces and is
re-radiated as heat

Earth's atmosphere acts like the glass of a greenhouse by permitting the Sun's energy to reach Earth's surface, then capturing some of the heat and preventing it from escaping into space. More and more heat is being trapped by the atmosphere due to increasing carbon dioxide and other greenhouse gases. This results in global warming.

being added to the atmosphere by human activity. It is estimated that humans add about 5.5 billion tons (5.0 billion metric tons) of carbon dioxide to the atmosphere each year by burning oil, coal, and natural gas. Carbon dioxide is also produced by cement manufacture. The result is that the extra gas is trapping more of the Sun's heat than normal. This is affecting worldwide temperatures.

Scientists estimate that the average temperature of Earth for the last ten thousand years has been about 59°F (15°C). Since 1850, however, Earth's average temperature has risen about 1°F (0.5°C). This wouldn't be too worrisome except it appears to be a trend that could reach as much as 8°F (4°C) in the next one hundred years.

GREENHOUSE EFFECT

We've all done it—jumped into a closed car on a hot, sunny day and jumped out again just as fast because we sat on a hot seat-belt buckle. While it is pleasantly warm outside, the inside temperature is sweltering! What is going on? Hot cars in summer get that way because of the greenhouse effect.

People use greenhouses to trap the Sun's heat and make better growing conditions for many plants. Sunlight enters through the glass and warms the soil in the growing beds. Instead of radiating back into space, the heat is trapped by the glass. Gradually, the temperature rises, helping the plants grow.

The windows of your car act like greenhouse glass. Sunlight hits the upholstery, seat belts, and steering wheel. They get hot, and the windows trap the heat. The temperature inside can easily reach a deadly 120°F (49°C) or more. That is why it is important to never leave a child or a pet in a closed car in the summer.

Different scientists come up with different temperature estimates, but it is clear that Earth is getting warmer.

It is difficult to be sure what will happen as Earth warms. Large segments of the Arctic ice cap could melt, leaving the Arctic Ocean ice free during the summer. A serious reduction in sea ice would hamper the ability of polar bears to hunt for food, therefore endangering their survival. The melting of the Antarctic and Greenland ice caps could be even more damaging. The loss of this ice would cause the sea level to rise as much as 20 feet (6 m). Many coastal cities and farmlands around the world would become flooded.

Scientists are reporting accelerated melting of the ice caps. Changing water temperatures could disrupt important ocean currents such as the Gulf Stream. European countries that depend upon warm Gulf Stream waters to moderate their winter temperatures would be faced with blistering cold winters and vastly increased use of fuel to keep warm.

The disruption of worldwide climates could also affect the world's food supply. Some areas would experience massive droughts while others might experience heavier rains. Stronger storms such as the killer hurricanes during the 2005 season would occur. More clouds would cover Earth at one time. Winds could become stronger. In a study by the journal *Conservation Biology*, scientists predicted that 25 percent of all the species of plant and animal life on Earth could become extinct in the next forty-five years due primarily to climate change.

Scientists are certain that global warming is taking place and that our survival will depend upon planetwide action. Yet, there is some uncertainty about how rapidly Earth is warming because humans are releasing much

Earth's average temperature was slightly less than 60°F (16°C) in 1880. By the year 2100, the average temperature will climb to between 62°F and 66°F (17°C and 19°C).

more into the atmosphere than just greenhouse gases. For example, tiny soot particles enter the air as a byproduct of burning fuels. These particles act like a sunscreen that blocks some of the Sun's heat. As South American countries, and nations such as China and India, increase their standard of living to become more industrialized and consume more products, their effect on global warming will also increase. Of all the environmental dangers we face, global warming is the most serious.

OZONE DEPLETION

Ozone depletion is one of the most potentially serious problems of the atmosphere. Unlike regular oxygen molecules, which contain two bonded atoms of oxygen, ozone molecules have three atoms of oxygen bonded together. Small quantities of ozone in the stratosphere serve as an important radiation shield for plants and animals on Earth's surface.

The Sun sends out dangerous UV radiation into space. Much of the UV sent to Earth is blocked by ozone. When stratospheric ozone absorbs the UV radiation, the ozone molecules are broken apart. The freed oxygen atoms eventually recombine into new ozone molecules. Without the ozone layer, more UV would reach Earth's surface, and this would cause damage to plants and animals. One of the potential consequences to humans of too much UV exposure is deadly skin cancer.

DRILLING FOR CLUES

While most scientists believe Earth's climate is getting warmer, there are many questions as to exactly what is happening and why. In fall 2004, scientists mounted the Arctic Coring Expedition (ACEX), an ambitious research project to extract a multimillion-year record of Earth's climate. Using an icebreaker and drilling rig ships, they drilled into an underwater mountain chain just 148 miles (238 km) from the North Pole. They extracted a 1,400-foot (430-meter)-long core from the mountain chain. It is being studied at the University of Bremen in Germany.

The team is trying to understand how the Arctic affects Earth's weather and climate. Layers of fossil plants and animals in cores give scientists clues about ocean and atmospheric temperature cycles and the effects that freezing and thawing of the Arctic ice pack had on them. (An ice pack is an expanse of ice chunks, clustered together in giant floating masses.) Currently, the Arctic ice pack is showing signs of melting. The core could provide important clues on how this melting will affect deepwater ocean currents and Earth's climate.

Early examination of the core has resulted in a startling discovery. About 55 million years ago, during a period of worldwide warming, the North Pole was ice-free and the Arctic Ocean water was about 40°F (20°C) warmer than it is today. It was nearly warm enough for swimming! Although the scientists are not sure what caused the warming, it could have started with massive volcanic eruptions releasing billions of tons (metric tons) of carbon dioxide into the atmosphere. The release would have led to a greenhouse effect that trapped more of the Sun's energy than normal and caused global warming.

69

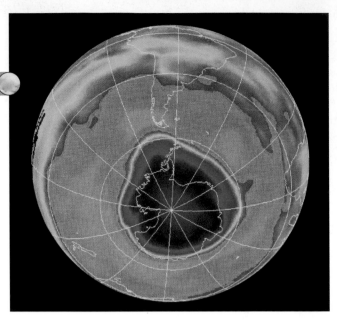

This satellite image of Earth was taken with a special camera that measures levels of atmospheric ozone. The dark violet and pink areas over Antarctica show a severe hole in the ozone layer.

Until recently, ozone molecules and UV radiation were in balance. Then, in the 1970s, it was learned that human-made chemicals were damaging the ozone layer. Around the world, gases called chlorofluorocarbons (CFCs) were being widely used in refrigerator and air-conditioner systems and for aerosol sprays. The CFCs were escaping into the atmosphere.

As long as the CFCs remained intact, they were harmless. However, scientists discovered that they were rising up in the atmosphere and breaking down, releasing chlorine atoms into the air. The chlorine was attacking the ozone and breaking apart the molecules. The balance between UV and ozone was disrupted, and the ozone layer started thinning. At times, the atmosphere over Antarctica showed ozone gaps, called ozone holes.

Eventually, enough scientific evidence was assembled that many nations of the world banned CFCs. Without the release of CFCs, it is hoped that the ozone layer might rebuild itself.

CONCLUSION
TAKING THE ATMOSPHERE FOR GRANTED

Air is something that we cannot survive without for more than a few minutes. The atmosphere continually changes and moves in a highly complex system. When something happens to the atmosphere in one place, it affects the entire atmosphere. Uneven heating of Earth's surface by the Sun creates wind. Winds move air and distribute heat and water around the planet. We are really only conscious of the atmosphere when the days are very hot or very cold or stormy.

It is understandable but dangerous to take the atmosphere for granted. Hundreds of years ago, when the world population was far smaller than it is today and technology was simple, there was not much humans could do to affect the atmosphere. That is not true anymore. Humans are clearly affecting Earth's climate. The dark streets, parking lots, and rooftops of large cities absorb so much of the Sun's energy that they become "heat islands" and create their own wind. Cement manufacture for road construction releases large quantities of carbon dioxide into the atmosphere. More roads mean more automobile traffic and more air pollution.

Worldwide demands for consumer goods are rising fast. To meet those demands, new factories that add more pollution to the atmosphere are being built. New industrial chemicals rise into the atmosphere and have unexpected effects on natural systems. Agricultural practices such as burning off forests to make more farmland add huge quantities of gas and particles to the atmosphere. The warming of the atmosphere is melting polar regions, altering ocean currents, intensifying destructive storms, producing droughts in some areas and flooding in others, and accelerating the extinction of animal and plant species.

The ultimate consequences of altering the atmosphere are hard to predict. Earth is a remarkable system that continually adjusts and rebalances itself, and the effects of human activity are relatively new in Earth's history. But it is clear that Earth needs our help. We need to reduce our impact on the atmosphere and other resources.

Each individual can help. Compact fluorescent lightbulbs for our lamps produce the same amount of light as regular bulbs but use far less energy and cost less to operate. Electric power generation is responsible for millions of tons (metric tons) of carbon dioxide being released into the atmosphere. We can drive less or use energy-efficient automobiles, such as the new gas and electric hybrid cars, that take less fuel and release less energy. We can buy fewer things and recycle paper, metal, plastic, and glass, which will save resources and reduce the amount of energy that is normally used when processing raw materials. We can encourage friends and family to do their part. We can contact our government representatives to let them know we expect action to reduce pollution. These are just a few of the ways we can make a difference.

The big question is, do we play it safe and look for ways to minimize our effect on the atmosphere or continue as we are and wait and see what happens? The answer to this question is a matter of life and breath.

GLOSSARY

air mass: a body of air that maintains as it travels uniform conditions, such as temperature or humidity. The air mass can extend hundreds or thousands of miles (kilometers) horizontally and sometimes reach as high as the stratosphere.

atmosphere: the portion of Earth that is dominated by the presence of gas and weather

atom: the smallest particle of any chemical element that still contains all the element's properties

biosphere: the thin zone on or near Earth's surface where living things reside

condensation: the process by which water vapor changes to liquid water by accumulating on cool surfaces to form drops

Coriolis effect: a result of Earth's rotation that causes moving air masses to move in a circular motion

density: the mass of an object divided by its volume

downdraft: a vertical wind that flows downward

elements: the different kinds of atoms that make up all matter

evaporation: changing from liquid water into water vapor

exosphere: the uppermost and thinnest part of the atmosphere where spacecraft orbit Earth

front: a narrow zone between warm and cold air masses

frost: ice that forms on cold surfaces that come in contact with moist air

gas: a state of matter that has no definite shape or volume

greenhouse gases: gases, such as carbon dioxide, in the atmosphere that tend to trap heat from the Sun similar to the way glass in greenhouses trap heat

hurricane: a swirling tropical storm with wind speeds exceeding 74 miles (120 km) per hour

hydrologic cycle: the cycle in which water from the atmosphere moves into the biosphere, lithosphere, and hydrosphere and back to the atmosphere

hydrosphere: Earth's oceans, lakes, and rivers

lithosphere: the solid rocky part of Earth's surface

matter: the atoms and molecules of which all physical objects are made

mesosphere: the layer of the atmosphere between the stratosphere and thermosphere where temperatures decrease with altitude

meteorology: the science of the atmosphere and weather

molecule: a combination of two or more atoms bonded together

ozone: a special form of the oxygen molecule consisting of three atoms of oxygen instead of the usual two

psi: the English unit for measuring pressure; stands for pounds per square inch

stratosphere: the layer of the atmosphere just above the troposphere where commercial jet airliners fly

sublimation: water changing from ice into water vapor or water vapor back into ice without becoming a liquid first

thermosphere: the layer of Earth's atmosphere above the mesosphere where air molecules are widely spaced and temperatures soar into the thousands of degrees

tornado: a powerful, funnel-shaped, swirling storm

transpiration: evaporation of the water released by plant leaves

tropical depression: a low-pressure zone over a tropical ocean that could intensify to become a hurricane

tropical storm: a tropical depression with wind speeds exceeding 39 miles (63 km) per hour

troposphere: the lowest layer of Earth's atmosphere where all of the weather we experience is located

updraft: a vertical wind blowing upward

water vapor: the gas form of water

weather: day-to-day events in the atmosphere

wind: a flow of air within the atmosphere

BIBLIOGRAPHY

Gore, Al. *An Inconvenient Truth*. New York: Rodale, 2006.

Hodgson, Michael. *Weather Forecasting*. Basic Essentials series. 2nd ed. Guilford, CT: Globe Pequot Press, 1999.

Lutgens, Frederick K, and Edward J. Tarbuck. *The Atmosphere: An Introduction to Meteorology*. 9th ed. Upper Saddle River, NJ: Prentice Hall, 2003.

NASA. "Earth's Atmosphere." *Liftoff to Space Exploration.* December 1, 1995. http://liftoff.msfc.nasa.gov/academy/space/atmosphere.html (September 19, 2006).

National Oceanic and Atmospheric Administration. "Global Warming." *NOAA*. February 3, 2006. http://www.ncdc.noaa.gov/oa/climate/globalwarming.html (September 19, 2006).

———. "National Hurricane Center." *NOAA*. September 19, 2006. http://www.nhc.noaa.gov/ (September 19, 2006).

———. "National Weather Service." *NOAA*. May 18, 2006. http://www.nws.noaa.gov/ (September 19, 2006).

———. "Tornadoes." *NOAA*. March 9, 2005. http://www.noaa.gov/tornadoes.html (September 19, 2006).

Rubin, Louis D. Sr., Jim Duncan, and Hiram J Herbert. *The Weather Wizard's Cloud Book: A Unique Way to Predict the Weather Accurately and Easily by Reading the Clouds*. Chapel Hill, NC: Algonquin Books, 1989.

Wallace, John M., and Peter V. Hobbs. *Atmospheric Science: An Introductory Survey*. 2nd ed. San Diego: Academic Press, 2006.

Williams, Jack. *The Weather Book: An Easy-to-Understand Guide to the USA's Weather*. 2nd ed. Rev. and updated. New York: Vintage , 1997.

FOR FURTHER INFORMATION

Books

Douglas, Paul. *Restless Skies: The Ultimate Weather Book*. New York: Sterling Publishing, 2004.

Harrison, C., and D. Krasnow. *Weather and Climate (Discovery Channel School Science)*. Milwaukee: Gareth Stevens Publishing, 2004.

Scholastic Atlas of Weather. New York: Scholastic Reference, 2005.

Silverstein, Alvin, Virginia Silverstein, and Laura Silverstein Nunn. *Global Warming*. Minneapolis: Twenty-First Century Books, 2003.

Weather. DK Eyewitness Books. New York: DK Publishing, 2004.

Woods, Michael, and Mary B. Woods. *Tornadoes*. Minneapolis: Lerner Publications Company, 2007.

Websites

Air Resources Board: Air Pollution and What You Can Do
http://www.arb.ca.gov/html/cando.htm
This state website provides specific activities for combating air pollution.

Discover Education
http://school.discovery.com/lessonplans/activities/weatherstation/
Learn about weather forecasting and how to build your own weather station with the plans on this website.

Natural Resources Defense Council: How To Fight Global Warming
http://www.nrdc.org/globalWarming/gsteps.asp
This website is sponsored by an environmental organization that provides suggestions on how to help reduce global warming.

NOAA Education
http://www.education.noaa.gov
This website provides links to information about weather and the environment for students and teachers.

U.S. Environmental Protection Agency
http://www.epa.gov
This website provides information and ideas on many atmosphere related topics.

INDEX

ABOUT THE AUTHOR

Gregory L. Vogt holds a doctor of education degree in curriculum and instruction from Oklahoma State University. He began his professional career as a science teacher. He later joined NASA's education programs teaching students and teachers about space exploration. He works in outreach programs for the Kennedy Space Center. He also serves as an educational consultant to Delaware North Parks Services of Spaceport and is the principal investigator for an educational grant with the National Space Biomedical Research Institute. Vogt has written more than seventy children's science books.

PHOTO ACKNOWLEDGMENTS